Real Families

Figuring out your family
and where you fit in

by Amy Lynch
illustrated by Carol Yoshizumi

Published by Pleasant Company Publications

Copyright © 2007 by American Girl, LLC

Questions or comments? Call 1-800-845-0005,
visit our Web site at **americangirl.com**, or write to Customer Service,
American Girl, 8400 Fairway Place, Middleton, WI 53562-0497.

Printed in China

07 08 09 10 11 12 RRDS 10 9 8 7 6 5 4 3 2 1

Editorial Development: Therese Kauchak Maring, Michelle Nowadly Watkins

Art Direction and Design: Chris Lorette David

Production: Kendra Schluter, Mindy Rappe, Jeannette Bailey, Judith Lary

Illustrations: Carol Yoshizumi

Photography: Fotosearch

Amy Lynch is a writer and speaker specializing in adolescent girls and family relationships. She is the author of *How Can You Say That? What to Say to Your Daughter When One of You Just Said Something Awful*, published by Pleasant Company Publications, and the founding editor of *Daughters* Newsletter.

This book is not intended to replace the advice of or treatment by physicians, psychologists, or other experts. It should be considered an additional resource only. Questions and concerns about mental or physical health should always be discussed with a doctor or other health-care provider.

Cataloging-in-Publication Data available from Library of Congress.

Dear Reader,

This book is about **you** and the people you are closest to—**your family.** They're the sisters or brothers who bug you sometimes but who are there for you when you're in a tight spot. They're the parents who wake you in the morning and give you a hug at night. They're the people who live with you and love you, who may embarrass you once in a while, but who believe in you more than anyone else on earth.

In this book you'll find ideas and activities to help you **understand** your family, **create memories** with them, and **negotiate solutions** when you disagree.

Most of all, as you read this book, you'll discover again and again how important YOU are to your family. They depend on you—unique and wonderful YOU—for the joy and liveliness you bring to the family. That's something you should always **feel good about.**

Your friends at American Girl

contents

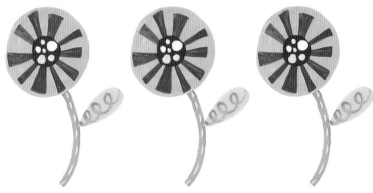

your family

Who tucked you in at night when you were little? Who remembers the first time you rode your bike or hit a softball? Your family.

Your family is *still* here for you. And that's great—because it's easier to take the changes life is throwing your way when you're surrounded by people who love you. The secret is learning to understand your family and the changes *they* are going through, too.

Family Basics

There's no magic recipe for a family. Families can be made up of all kinds of ingredients. **And when those ingredients are mixed together, each family comes out in its own unique way.**

The family in your life today might be made up of . . .

- two sets of grandparents
- two parents
- your brother
- and your dog, Frank.

Or it might consist of . . .

- one grandmother
- your parents
- a stepparent
- your brother and stepsister
- and a new baby half brother.*

You may live with your family all in one home, or you may split your time between your parents' homes. It doesn't matter— you're all still FAMILY.

*A *stepsibling* is the child of your stepparent from a different relationship.
 A *half sibling* shares one of your parents.

List the names of your family members here, and write one positive trait that you like about each person.

Name: _____

Something I like about this person: _____

_____

Name: _____

Something I like about this person: _____

_____

Name: _____

Something I like about this person: _____

_____

Name: _____

Something I like about this person: _____

_____

Name: _____

Something I like about this person: _____

_____

Name: _____

Something I like about this person: _____

_____

Your Role

Your parents, brothers, and sisters spend more time with you than anyone else you know. How do you act when you're with them? Find out by taking this quiz. **Put a check next to the answer that describes you best.**

1

When I have to share the computer or the phone, I . . .

    a. would rather go away and come back later—when I can have them all to myself.

    b. work out deals for sharing ("What if I use the computer for 30 minutes now and you use it for an hour after dinner?").

    c. sometimes get in an argument.

    d. take whatever time I can get and work very intensely when it is my turn.

    e. usually ask a parent to work it out.

2

During meals, I . . .

    a. mostly eat in silence, or talk quietly.

    b. help my younger brother or sister with his or her food.

    c. disagree with my parents about what I ought to eat.

    d. get really excited telling stories about my day.

    e. feel happy that we take time to eat together as a family.

3

My usual mood at home is . . .

    a. spaced out. I am in my own world and may not seem to pay attention to what's going on.

    b. focused. I like planning things and getting them accomplished.

    c. impatient. My family can be so irritating.

    d. happy. I'm usually ready for anything!

    e. loving. Hugs are absolutely my favorite part of the day.

4 At bedtime, I . . .

a. head straight to my room. I like the quiet time.

b. am totally organized for the next morning, with my clothes laid out and ready.

c. sometimes think about apologizing if I did something I regret during the day.

d. am wide awake. It's hard for me to let go of the excitement of the day.

e. am snuggly and quiet.

Look back over your answers.

• If you answered mostly **a**'s, you treasure privacy. Even though you may enjoy being the "strong, silent" member of the family, be sure to speak up when you have thoughts or feelings that need to be heard.

• If you answered mostly **b**'s, you have can-do confidence. Pay attention to having fun, too. Spend time with your family just hanging out and talking. They need your warmth and affection as much as they need your organizational skills!

• If you answered mostly **c**'s, your strong feelings make you decisive and a leader. Your passionate personality can stimulate your family! Just be sure determination doesn't become bossiness. If it does, apologize. Your family will appreciate it, and you'll be proud of your leadership skills.

• Mostly **d** answers show you have plenty of get-up-and-go. If other people in your family have similar energy levels, you can be active together! If not, think about balance. Some family members may need gentleness from you.

• The **e**'s you chose show you have an extra-loving heart. Are you the person others come to for comfort? What a wonderful gift to your family! Remember to also allow yourself to say "not now" if you are tired or unhappy. Your own needs are important—and other family members need the satisfaction of giving out warm fuzzies, too!

"They Think I Am . . ."

Pretend you happen to overhear your mother or father on the phone describing you to someone you've never met. What would he or she say? Don't think about this too hard—just jot down three or four words.

What are some good words your brother or sister would use to describe you?

When you were younger, you would have listed *different* words than those you just wrote. Look at the words on your lists. Put an X next to words that are different from what you would have written a year ago. Those words show *you're changing.*

big
TRUTH

You are changing. In fact, between the ages of 8 and 12, you change more quickly than anybody else in your family, unless there's a baby crawling around your house.

When *you* were a baby, you went from crawling to walking in only a few months. Now, for the second time in your life, your brain and body change so fast that you may feel, think, and act very differently in only weeks.

Looking Back

How have you changed during this last year? Maybe you joined a team or a club, discovered you like to speak French, or learned to boogie board.

In horseback riding I can canter and jump now. Those things took courage to learn.
Courtney, age 11

I moved last year and that changed me. Now I know I can deal with new things, even if at first I don't like them.
Katie, age 10

I'm at a much more advanced reading level than I was last year, and I learned to do a back walkover.
Liana, age 9

• Skate • Ski • Play tennis, basketball, or soccer • Solve
gh problems and solve them • Play an instrument • Organize
alone • Ride my bike faster than before • Earn money • Rea
Solve
ganiz
y • R
ese
Spe
ketb
inst
re
aca
sist
hy t
em
fas
m
pu
e •
ar
r
tl
r
l

**Three things I can do now that
I couldn't do a year ago:**

1. _____

   _____

   _____

2. _____

   _____

   _____

3. _____

   _____

   _____

Parents Change, Too

One of the great things about parents is that they always want to be there for you. But *because* they are always there, it can be easy to overlook that your parents are changing, too.

When was the last time you noticed something new about your mother or father? Maybe one of them surprised you by learning another language or being in a play.

Explore the ways your parents or stepparents are changing by putting a check beside the things that are true.

One of my parents or stepparents . . .

☐ has found a new hobby or sport.

☐ has taken a different job.

☐ has divorced or remarried.

☐ exercises more than he or she used to.

☐ exercises less than he or she used to.

☐ has had a parent who was ill or who recently died.

☐ is planning a vacation.

☐ laughs more these days.

☐ acts more serious these days.

☐ recently celebrated a big anniversary or birthday.

Green Light?

By now you understand that you are changing, and fast—so fast that you're like a traffic light stuck on green for go.

This is exciting for you! But your mom or dad may act like a yellow light or even a red one, signaling for you to slow down or even stop.

More than anything, **your parents want to keep you safe.** If you want to ride your bike to the store or go to a movie with your friends, you may think, *Fun!* But your parents may say, "I don't know about this." Then again, they may say, "Go for it!"

No matter which signal your parents give you,

nothing seems the same as it was last year—or maybe even last week.

Every time *you* change, your family changes in some way, too. See if these examples fit your family.

- You understand jokes now, so your parents tell you more jokes.

- You are stronger, so your big sister or brother plays basketball against you more seriously.

- You are more responsible, so your family depends on you more.

- You are better at making decisions and taking care of yourself, so your parents let you make more choices.

Action!

Your family life is kind of like a movie. Every day, the story-line is changing and characters are developing. Some scenes may make you laugh and others may make you feel like crying.

But what's happening now is only one part of the ongoing story. Learning to communicate better with your family—by talking and keeping your minds and hearts open—can help you enjoy the show, no matter what happens in the next scene!

getting along

Sometimes the people closest to our hearts are the ones we take for granted the most. Maybe that's because we assume they will always be around. Do you think that's *really* a good idea?

Here are 27 ways to help everybody in your family feel just a little happier and know that they matter to you.

1 Start the day gently. Are you half asleep in the a.m.? You're not alone. Give everybody in your family a little extra understanding in the morning. They're sleepwalking just like you!

2 Share YOURSELF. Your parents miss you if you don't spend time with them. Surprise them! Take time now and then to hang out with them. Play a game, take a walk, or bake a cake—together.

3

Lend a hand. Did you know that parents do nine or ten chores for every one chore a kid does? So clear the table, scrape the scraps, and toss the trash. Doing chores without being asked? Bonus points!

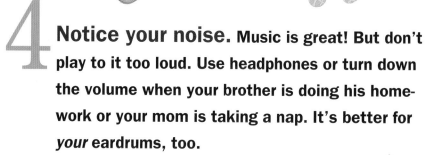

4 **Notice your noise.** Music is great! But don't play to it too loud. Use headphones or turn down the volume when your brother is doing his homework or your mom is taking a nap. It's better for *your* eardrums, too.

5

Try to do your homework early. The closer it is to bedtime, the harder it is to get the work done, and the harder it is for your parents to help.

6 Think small. **Don't forget the wee ones. Little brothers and sisters need lots of help. Be there for them** with hugs, games, and peanut-butter-and-jelly sandwiches!

7 **Do roommate research.** Your family members are like roommates! If you have brothers or sisters in college, ask them what special things they do to get along with *their* roomies. Maybe the same ideas will work at home.

8 **Schedule it.** Dance lessons, scouts, soccer practice, babysitting, and overnights—you have a million places to go. Put your schedule on the family calendar ahead of time. Be part of the plan.

9 **Stash your stuff.** Keeping your things in your room helps the family stay on the go. And nobody will trip over your backpack in the hallway.

10

Live a little! Every family has traditions, like singing goofy songs or eating spaghetti every Sunday night. Join the fun, even if you're not in the mood. Traditions keep us connected, and they lift our spirits.

11

Put it away. Everything has a place. The tape lives on the desk and the hammer lives in the toolkit, so after you use them, put them back. That way, *everybody* will be able to find them the next time.

Here I am!

12

Beat a retreat. Feeling moody? Try not to take it out on your family. When even *you* know you're crabby, do something that helps you feel soothed, like playing with your pet, taking a warm bath, or reading a good book.

13 Get your ZZZs. Resist starting something energizing, such as a video game or a pillow fight, right before it's time to snooze . . . even if it's tempting!

14 Joke gently. Some people in your family probably can make a joke and take a joke, but not everyone can. And even those who *can* can't take jokes all the time. Respect the feelings family members have about teasing and tickling. They'll be more likely to respect your feelings, too.

15 Be sympathetic. When your dad is sick or your sister gets cut from the team, they'll need you to be there for them 100 percent. Let the feelings flow. Your family will feel better just knowing that you care.

> I'm sorry you feel bad. What can I do to help you feel better?

16 Don't like it? Don't complain. Solve the problem. If the family is planning to eat something for dinner that you don't like, try asking ahead of time if you can substitute something else. Asking at the table is too late!

17 Walk the dog. Do your share of critter care. Pet the cat, feed the fish, and don't ignore the iguana (even if he ignores you).

My dog is like family. I remember washing him when he was a puppy. I took him in the shower and then wrapped him in a towel. It makes me feel good to help out around the house. I know my mom depends on me.

Hannah, age 10

18

Say **"Please"** and **"thanks."**
Little things count, and these little words
really work. No wonder some people call
them magic!

19

Meet and greet. **"Have a great day"**
and **"welcome home"** can be real pick-
me-ups for the person walking through the
door. These may be the best words your
mom will hear all day, especially since they
come from you.

20

Give healthy hugs. Did you know hugs can make us
healthier? People who get plenty of hugs tend to get
sick less often than those who don't. So share hugs
with your family and spread the good feeling around.
Remember, you always have the right to say NO to hugs
and cuddles if you don't want them.

21 **Not now, but later.** When you ask someone in the family for help or for a favor, try asking for it *later* instead of right this minute. Then the answer is more likely to be "yes."

22 **Make a list.** Hate running errands with your parents? Make the job easier by writing out a list and checking things off as you get them done. This helps your parents stay organized, too.

23

Phone home.
If you promised to
call your parents
at a certain time,
phone home and let
them know every-
thing is going just
as planned.

Hey, Mom, guess what?
We won the game! Now we're
going out with Coach
for dinner.

Hi, Dad. Christine and I are
leaving the movie with her
mom now. See you later.

24

Stay in touch. When your parents travel
away from home, send an e-mail or a letter to
let them know you miss them. The trip will seem
shorter to them and the distance closer when
they feel your love.

25

Be there for B-days. Birthdays are **BIG** days no matter what your age. When your parents or siblings have birthdays, do your part to make the day special. Light the candles, and help the person you are celebrating shine!

26

Extend yourself. When your grandparents come to visit or Thanksgiving rolls around, you may have to give up time with your friends. But being gracious pays off— your aunts, uncles, and grandparents can tell you great family stories you never knew!

27

Roll with it. Your dad whistles when you're trying to study? Your sister borrows your books and forgets to return them? That's just life, and sometimes it's not worth bothering about. Relax and let a few things slide. It's all part of getting along with the cast of characters you call *family*!

family first aid

You can't always prevent family misunderstandings (nobody can!) but you *can* do your part to help clear the air.

big
TRUTH

Families fight. It's normal.

Your family members will not get along perfectly all the time, unless they are one of the following:

        a. mannequins

        b. robots

        c. fairy-tale characters

If your family is made up of real live humans, then family feelings *will* get out of control from time to time—even though you love one another with all your hearts. So what should you do when things get rough? Learn to help solve problems. If you do that, it'll be a sure sign you're growing up.

Let's Make a Deal

You may not realize that you already know how to negotiate, or help find a solution that works for everyone involved in a disagreement. But you do. Whether you're the oldest child, an only child, the youngest in the family, or anywhere in between—you work out agreements with family members all the time.

Think about the past few days. What deals did you make with people in your family? Did everybody get what he or she wanted? Did you have any arguments that could have been solved through negotiation? List a few of each here.

Deals I made:

_____

_____

_____

_____

_____

Arguments that could have been deals:

_____

_____

_____

_____

_____

45

Alike or Different?

Figuring out how you are similar to—and different from—the people in your family can help you understand them . . . **and understand how to get along with them.** Maybe *you* have a quick temper, but your sister hardly ever gets upset. Maybe you and your mother both laugh when you're nervous. Think about it!

Ready for a challenge? At the top of the next page, write down the names of three people in your family.

Get set. Find a timer and set it for three minutes. During that three minutes, you're going to think of all the ways you are similar to, and different from, those people. You don't need to write full sentences, just enough words to make the idea clear. You can write about physical attributes (you both have green eyes), artistic tastes (neither of you like opera music), or emotional things (you both cry in movies or yell when you're mad).

Go! Start the timer, and turn the page.

Fill in as many spaces as you can in only three minutes.

Name: _____

How we're alike: _____

_____

_____

How we're different: _____

_____

_____

Name: _____

How we're alike: _____

_____

_____

How we're different: _____

_____

_____

Name: _____

How we're alike: _____

_____

_____

How we're different: _____

_____

_____

When three minutes are up, stop and count your answers. Whose "alike list" is the longest? Whose "different list" is the longest?

The person most like you may be the one you get along with best. The person most different from you may be someone you have trouble understanding sometimes. Getting along with that person may require patience and your very best negotiating skills. Either way, you can learn from your lists!

Word Power

Words are powerful things, whether you're working things out with a parent, stepparent, brother, sister, stepsibling, or naughty dog. Say the words below out loud. Pause after each word to notice how it makes your body feel.

Chances are, saying these words made you feel something. The kinder words—sweetie, dear, and honey—may have given you a little smile inside or made you feel positive. The unkind words—klutz, stupid, worthless, and loser—may have made you utter a mental "ouch."

Just as *these* words made you feel good or bad, the words *you* use affect the emotions of everyone in your family. When you say loving words or fighting ones, the "emotional temperature" at your house changes instantly!

Translation, Please

Angry words often mean more than one thing and can stem from more than one feeling. The words below are good examples. Draw lines from the words on the left to their most likely meanings on the right. Then look at the red words to see what feelings might cause someone to burst out with these phrases.

Words

1. You're not the boss of me!

2. You lied to me!

3. Shut up!

4. You're stupid!

Meanings

a. Something changed, and I don't like it! CONFUSED DISAPPOINTED

b. I can't deal with this right now. Leave me alone. STRESSED OUT

c. I feel so bad about myself that I have to tell you you're no good, too. ASHAMED AFRAID

d. I'm not in control. HELPLESS POWERLESS

The answers are on the next page.

Mean words are never O.K., and there is no excuse for anyone to be cruel to you. But if you understand that **lots of different feelings may cause someone to use angry words,** it may help you figure out what's going on. And *that* makes it easier to talk with some-one when you're trying to work things out.

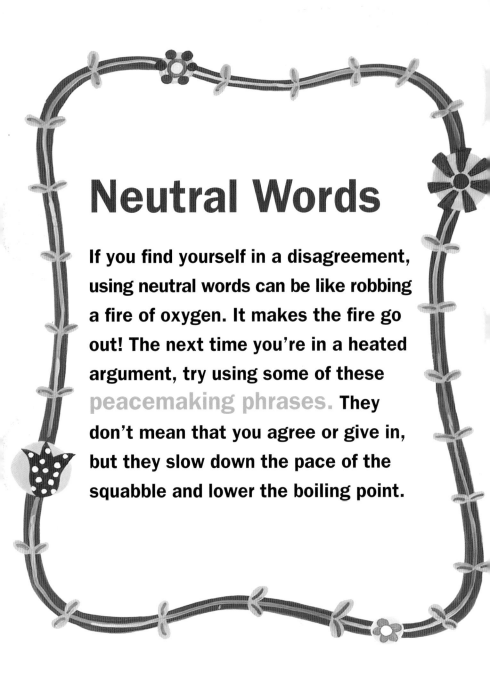

Neutral Words

If you find yourself in a disagreement, using neutral words can be like robbing a fire of oxygen. It makes the fire go out! The next time you're in a heated argument, try using some of these peacemaking phrases. They don't mean that you agree or give in, but they slow down the pace of the squabble and lower the boiling point.

5 Ways to Chill Out

1

Just breathe. Deep breathing will soothe and steady you. If someone says something that gets you riled, before you say anything back, take two

l..o..n..g,

s..l..o..w

breaths.

This alone can take the wind out of an argument.

2 Understand that you're "mad all over." Getting angry affects more than your heart and your head. Your whole body feels it! When you're angry, your heart beats faster, your muscles tense, your breathing speeds up, and your brain produces "angry" chemicals. It can take at least 20 minutes for all of that to go away. Until then, some part of your body is still mad! Give yourself time to calm down and work through your emotions.

3 ## Calm down by getting physical.

Can't stop an argument? Say, "You know, I'm feeling _____" and fill in the emotion you feel. Then explain: "I need time to calm down." Leave the scene, and get moving! Shoot hoops hard, take a fast run, jump in a pool, jump on your bike, or climb a tree. Use your muscles to calm your mind.

4

Ask questions. When you feel calmer, ask yourself some questions about what happened. This gets the thinking part of your brain working rather than the feelings part. Writing your answers in your diary may help you think more clearly.

5

Have some girl gumption. If you argue with someone you love, odds are you'll feel pretty awful about it. But part of living in a family is learning to stand up for yourself. If you have *gumption*, it means you're willing to take a step, be bold, or—in this case— **speak up.** If your brother teases you too harshly, say so. If you got blamed for something that you didn't do, say so.

You don't have to yell to do this. You just have to keep saying how your feel and what you need until somebody hears you! If things get tense, **be patient and keep talking.** This is what it means to stand on your own two feet.

Talking It Out

Take two! Try these conversation starters when you want to come to an understanding with someone.

Read body language. You may not need to say anything to get a conversation rolling. Look into the other person's eyes. If you see love there, you can offer a hug. Chances are, that will naturally get the talk flowing!

Brainstorm. Ask the other person to brainstorm with you about some ways you can avoid having the same quarrel again. Two brains are better than one— at least, they are when they're not in an argument!

I have a sister who is five years old. If we get in a fight and I want to make up, I offer to play with her. She loves that.

Skylar, age 10

Saying Sorry

Only *you* know in your heart if you meant to say something mean to your parent, steparent, brother, sister, step-sibling, or that naughty dog.

If you didn't, don't apologize just to be nice—that would be dishonest. On the other hand, if you did something that hurt someone's feelings, come clean! Apologizing will help you—and the other person—feel better, and then you can start fresh.

Keep the apology short and simple. Just say you're sorry for what you did or said. Resist the urge to make excuses or explain *why* you did what you did. That way, **the apology won't be about YOU, but about the person who was hurt.**

About that lump in your throat . . . Sometimes apologizing can be embarrassing, even painful. If you need courage, give yourself a little time—but don't avoid apologizing.

Your Personal First-Aid Kit

Some families have quiet disagreements; others have big, loud clashes. Big or little, family conflicts can make our hearts hurt. Put a checkmark next to the ideas you can use to take care of yourself when there is tension in your family. Add your own ideas in the blank spaces.

I can . . .

☐ remind myself that even when we argue, we still love one another.

☐ cry and let my feelings out.

☐ ask for a comforting hug.

☐ move my body and get physical.

☐ talk to a good friend about my feelings.

☐ ask for help from a loving adult.

☐ write or draw how I feel.

☐ get outside and soak up some nature.

☐ _____

☐ _____

☐ _____

get close . . . and closer!

The secret to getting closer to your family is being curious about their stories, their dreams, and their hearts. Have fun together! Here are some activities you can do that will make you smile—and help you get to know one another even better.

1

Get the scoop. Think you know your family well? Complete the sentences below by circling a family member and filling in the blank. Next, become a reporter. Interview your family to see how many of the questions you got right.

1. One of my mom's/dad's favorite books is _____
_____

2. My sister's/brother's favorite room in our house is
_____

3. One of my mom's/dad's favorite movies is _____
_____

4. When my grandmother was a girl, she lived in
_____

5. When my other grandmother was a girl, she lived in
_____

6. At my age, my mom/dad wanted to be a _____
_____ when she/he grew up.

7. If my brother/sister could travel anywhere in the world, it would be _____

8. One of the biggest adventures my mom/dad ever had was

_____

9. One of my mom's/dad's closest friends is named _____

_____

10. My sister's/brother's best part of the day is _____

_____

11. My mom's/dad's favorite kind of music is _____

_____

Scoring

9 or more correct

Congratulations! You already listen closely to the people in your family. If you were the contestant on a family quiz show, you could win first prize!

5–8 correct

You've been doing a good job paying attention to details in your family. With a little work, you could write an encyclopedia of family trivia.

4 or fewer

There's a whole world of fun family facts out there to discover. The more you know about your family members, the better you'll understand them—and that can mean more closeness and good times at home.

2

Celebrate your specialness!

Most families have quirky members with quirky traits. Strange as it sounds, those are things that can make families closer.

My dad is a terrible singer. When he sings, my sister and I start singing as loud as we can so we can't hear him, but then he sings louder. Then my mom starts yelling at us all to be quiet. The weird thing is we do this every day!

Madeline, age 11

Our dog, Rusty, makes this barky sound, and my mom talks back to him. Then he talks back to her. They even talk about the weather!

Annie, age 10

My mom gets excited over nothing. Today she started dancing because she got a book about flowers. It was crazy.

Kellye, age 12

My aunt always says, "Cute, cute, cute!" when she likes something. She says it three times, never once or twice—always three.

Rhonda, age 11

3

Enjoy the nighttime neighborhood.
If you live in a place where you can walk
at night, ask your family to take an evening stroll. The world feels totally different in the dark, and there's a special
closeness that comes from seeing your
street at bedtime. Besides, a walk in the
evening is a good time for sharing stories
of the day or memories from the past.
Don't forget a flashlight!

Share your dreams. When you wake up, tell the story of your dream to your parent or sister quickly before you forget! Does anybody in your family have ideas about what your dream might mean? Are there clues in the dream that can help you solve a daytime problem? If morning is too busy, write down your dream and share it in the evening. Ask your family what they dreamed about, too!

5 **Join family members while they do something they love.** Watch hockey with your brother, or listen to jazz with your mom. Bake bread or hit golf balls with your dad. Even if it's not your favorite thing to do, it will draw you closer. Maybe next time, they'll do what *you* love to do—with you!

6 Play by the numbers. Grab any family member, or divide your family into two teams. Write the list below on another sheet of paper so that you have two copies. Yell "One, two, three— go!" and see which team can find the answers most quickly.

When you're done, see if both teams got the same answers. The team with most correct answers gets to take the other team out for ice cream!

Number of jars of peanut butter in the house	
Number of windows in the house	
Number of pets in the family	
Number of telephones the family has (count cell phones, too!)	
Number of shoes in the front closet	
Number of steps leading up to the front door	
Number of bicycles in the family	
Number of drawers in the kitchen	
Number of rugs in the house (count the doormats, too!)	

7

Share a read. Have you read a good book recently? Your family might enjoy lots of the books you like, too. Loan a book to your mom, dad, sister, or brother. Talking about exciting plot twists or comparing what you thought about a book can make for great conversations.

What would you have done in her place?

Could you believe the ending?

I cried in that part, too.

8 Send signals. Speak your own private language by making up family-only code words or signals.

A tug on your ear could mean "Look at that." Saying "FHB" when guests are over for dinner could be code for "family, hold back" so that there will plenty of food for guests. But be careful about using family signals in public. They can give you incurable giggles!

Once we were at the zoo and couldn't find the bathroom. We also couldn't find the elephants. So now when we say, "Where is the elephant?" it really means something else!

Fran, age 9

If something comes up at dinner that my mom doesn't want me to hear, she says, "Come help me with the dishes." Everybody laughs because we all know what she means!

Victoria, age 10

9

Get game crazy. Talk with your family about regularly setting aside an evening to play games. You could call it Find Family Fun Night! On FFF Night, turn off the computer, TV, and cell phones, and break out a game. Teach a younger sibling how to play something new. Other times, choose a game based on luck, so even little sibs will have a chance to win.

10

Make it official! Schools have official songs. States have official birds. Why not your family? Brainstorm with other family members to fill in the blanks below:

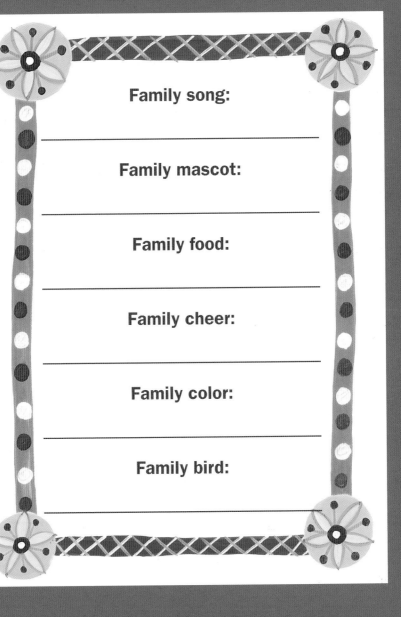

Family song:

_____

Family mascot:

_____

Family food:

_____

Family cheer:

_____

Family color:

_____

Family bird:

_____

11

Draw your family flag here. Include symbols, words, and colors that represent your family to you.

12

Look into the future. Make a list of things that are true right now about you and your family. You can also make predictions for the coming year. Seal the list in an envelope marked "Open Next Year." Pack it away with the holiday decorations. Read the list together next year to see how things have changed!

13

Plant memories. Plant a tree or a bush together to mark a family event. **Graduating from elementary school? That's a big event. Anniversaries and birthdays are, too. So are sad times such as losing a grandparent. Your family will feel connected on the day you plant the tree and every time you see it all year round.**

14

Play "Best Thing, Worst Thing." At the dinner table, ask each person to tell the best thing that happened that day. Then ask each person to tell the worst part of his or her day. If people are in a joking mood, have a contest to see who had the very best and very worst days. If your family is feeling serious, simply share your stories. Either way, you'll feel closer than you did before!

15

Get tangled up in love. Find a ball of yarn or string. Ask your family to stand in a circle. Start by holding the end of the string and tossing the ball to someone else. (It will unwind as you toss it.) After you toss the ball, say something good about the person who caught it.

Next, have the catcher toss the ball to someone else—still holding on to part of the string—and say what he or she appreciates about *that* person. Keep tossing the ball around the circle until the string is unwound. What a web of good feelings you made!

16

Cheer for the home team. What are the biggest challenges your family members are going through? Is your brother having a hard time with math? Has your mom been spending long hours at the office? Leave a note cheering him or her on. If you have time, make a banner or a sign using bright, energizing colors. Knowing you believe in them will help your family members face their troubles and reach their goals.